ROBERTS' RULES

OF

LESBIAN DATING

Shelly Roberts

Spinsters Ink
Duluth, MN

Roberts' Rules of Lesbian Dating © 1998 by Shelly Roberts

Published by Spinsters Ink
32 E. First St., #330
Duluth, MN 55802-2002, USA

First Edition May 1998, All Rights Reserved
10-9-8-7-6-5-4-3-2-1

Cover Design: Virginia Sutton   Book Design: Sara Sinnard & Erin Scott, Sarin Creative

Production: Liz Brissett   Marian Hunstiger   Amy Strasheim
               Helen Dooley   Claire Kirch   Liz Tufte
               Joan Drury   Ryan Petersen   Nancy Walker
               Emily Gould   Kim Riordan

Library of Congress Cataloging-in-Publication Data
Roberts, Shelly 1943 –
       Roberts' rules of lesbian dating / Shelly Roberts — 1st ed.
               p.   cm.
       On cover: 3
ISBN 1-883523-25-7 (alk. paper)
1. Lesbians – United States – Humor 2. Lesbianism – United States – Humor
3. Dating (Social customs) — United States — Humor.
I. Title.
PN6231.L43R655   1998
818'.5407—dc21
                                                                      98–18496
                                                                      CIP

Printed in Canada on recycled acid-free paper.

To Annette, Audrey, Carole, Charlotte, Christine, Cris, Denise, Eileen, Erin, Hazel, June, Jenifer, Karin, Kris, Laura, Mary-Helen, Melissa, Robin, Roz, Sue, Susan, Tanya, Tina B, Val, and Yvonne: my ad hoc dating advisory panel. To Valerie, for my first practice at doing dating in a very long time, for her patience and her wit. To Robert, who lent me his house in Atlanta to write this when I needed to run away from home. To Every Lesbian who ever found the Rock of Gibraltar in her throat while trying to utter the simple phrase, "Would you like to go to a movie?" And to all the single lesbians in Atlanta and the world for the research I still have yet to do.

Lesbian Dating Is Not

Ask any random lesbian you happen to encounter on any street corner of any town in the U.S. about lesbian dating, and you'll get a fairly limited, but predictable, range of responses:

Outright laughter.

Complete denial.

Abject awe.

Or something about a U-Haul.

You see, most lesbians don't believe in lesbian dating. Well, not for themselves. Many lesbians believe in the *idea* of dating, in the *abstract concept* of dating, even in the *probability of*, and *necessity for* dating (for some OTHER people). But few will admit ever actually having experienced the awful phenomenon personally.

If you listen to what they say, most lesbian couples will tell you that friends of friends introduced them just at the precise instant when they were each contemplating leaving previous involvements, so their feet never touched the dating floor.

A Contradiction In Terms.

Or, after eight, sixteen, twenty-four years, they are still with the perfect woman they met in college, life is still extraordinary, and they are expecting to go on living happily-ever-after until the day they die at precisely the same instant and are buried side-by-side in a candle ceremony by caring, coupled friends in similar circumstances.

Such is the nearly universal terror of lesbian dating.

"I mean, WHO would you find out there?" you can hear the ladies protest. "All the good ones are already taken. And quickly too."

Given how often lesbians trade one partner for another without ever having to buy soup for one or their own dishcloths, it isn't surprising that there is a widely held lesbian belief that lesbian dating doesn't exist. Or that it's fringe behavior reserved for the unfortunate few without good enough friends to get them properly fixed up.

What they really mean is that *they don't know how.*

Like so much other lesbiana, our beliefs about our behaviors stem from what we learned in other lifetimes, in heterosexual galaxies far, far away.

Most women's (let alone lesbians') early experiences of dating are from the victim side. Little girls sitting patiently by their phones waiting for some selecting male to deem them worthy.

No wonder we don't like it. It's an awful experience to be drawing from. And one that lesbians are often hard put to surmount, particularly given our natural predilection for members of our own gender, and therefore, not having such a great straight dating track record.

But the good news is:
Lesbian dating lives!

There are so many more of us out there now. Baby Boomer lesbians coming out in unheard-of numbers are passing into and out of coupledom with such frequency now that they are changing the face of lesbian dating.

Lesbian dating lives, of course, where it always lived: in dingy, dark lesbian bars where flipping a quarter onto the pool table used to be considered a dating request.

But it also lives in increasingly occurring seminars on how-to-do-it. Lesbian therapists (a redundancy?) are adding a whole new category to their repertoire. "How To Do Dating" is the single fastest growing segment in the how-to-be-a-lesbian marketplace. Some smart, single, nontherapeutic lesbians who want to meet interesting single women are creating dating seminars, just so they can sit at the front of the circle.

Lesbian dating lives in the supermarket, at the laundromat, at the political rally, at the fund-raiser, at the bookstore, and in whole new ways in the workplace.

In fact, the workplace is getting unimagined support from straight allies. Office yentas, without bias, are now just as likely to fix up their lesbian coworkers as to try to make matches between their hetero workmates. And single lesbian cousins, aunts, and sisters are no longer safe from the plaintive refrain, "There's this really nice woman in the office . . . just broke up with her . . . um . . . um . . . would you like . . . ?"

There is a growing reserve of more than middle-aged women who now find that the ways they are set in seem to suit them just fine, thank you very much, and they aren't looking to add another ego to their household. They like the idea of taking charge of their own romantic lives in ways that haven't existed before. With interesting, and innovative results: long-distance dating; Internet dating; noncommitment interaction; cuddle-buddying; win-win dating; once-a-week dating; dinner-club dating.

Some of the rules are the same ones dating has always had, with slight skewing for same sex. But many are brand new. Because, as always, we need our own rules, so we make them up as we go along.

The Dating Rules

Brand New At This?	2
Putting The Past Behind You	42
Getting On With It	78
Just For The Fun Of It	112
Looking For Love	144
Is There No End To This?	170

Roberts' First Rule
is *always* the same:
it is never a good idea to ask
someone to marry you
before the first date.

Brand New At This?

What if you've never done lesbian dating before? You're a political lesbian who now wants a real girlfriend? Or your very first girlfriend left you to figure this out alone? Or, after several relationships in a row, all the serial has poured out of your box of monogamy?

There's no one waiting in the wings. What do you do now?

You start with the lesbian dating basics:

What To Bring:

✔ A Toothbrush

✔ A Date

✔ Enough Money

✔ Training Wheels

✔ Your Therapist's #

✔ Your Medical Records

✔ A Complete List of Your Boundaries

✔ Your Screwed-Up Courage

DATING IS:

What you do while
you're waiting for your
next girlfriend.

Lesbian dating
is not a
contradiction
in terms.

A lesbian date
usually lasts
at least three years.

A lesbian
one-night stand,
on the other hand,
is over in mere months.

On the first date,
DON'T
get anything
tattoo'd.

Or
pierced.

Do not
sleep with
your last
ex.

DO NOT
sleep with
your last
ex.

Do NOT
sleep with
your LAST
EX!

Oh, all right!
Just that once.

You will put more food in
your refrigerator than you or
your date can eat.

Most of it will become
a decay experiment before
your next date.

Most of your coupled friends
will pity you.
Except for the ones
who envy you.

Those people are
very often married
to each other.

Ask to see
the results
of her blood test
first.

In the new reality,
getting tested together
is considered
a date.

She who is the most
assertive gets to
pick the movie.

Going out to dinner
is the only way
some single lesbians
ever get to eat a meal.

Sex
changes
everything.

You will learn
to love
lube and latex.

She can't say "Yes"
if you don't ask her
to dance.

Never loan a date
more money than
she is old.

When inviting
a lesbian out,
it is necessary
to use the actual word "date."

Especially if you
want her to know
that it is one.

It isn't necessary to accept
a date just because
someone asked.

It isn't fair to keep dating
someone just because
there isn't someone else.

It's more than a "good idea" to
ask friends to fix you up.
It's necessary.

Just remember to tell them
who or what you want
if you don't want
to be too disappointed.

Lesbian Dating
is a full-time job.

Yes, it *would* be a whole lot easier just to give up and stay home.

It is never too early
to find out if she has a
concealed weapons permit.

Or if her ex does.

Don't flirt with any one
else's girlfriend.

Period.

Like puppies,
lesbian dates tend
to follow you home.

If you don't want
to marry her,
don't ask her
to the movies.

Looks aren't nearly
as important
as confidence.

DATING IS:

That brief period
between long stretches
of talking to yourself.

Putting The Past Behind You

It's over. She's gone. Omigod, she's gone!

You might have been the New Jersey State Lesbian Dating Champ before you met her and have the Ms. Congeniality trophy to prove it. But for a time after a breakup, post-relationship regulations apply.

You just have to remember to apply them to yourself and to apply yourself to them:

What To Bring:

✔ A New Set Of Realities

✔ A New Attitude

✔ Your Power

✔ A Grip

✔ A Clue

✔ A Very Short Memory

✔ A Ray Of Hope

✔ Your Therapist's #

It is better to break up
with your current lover
before
sleeping with your date.

It isn't statistically likely.
But it *is* better.

A date
is
an audition.

Not

a

therapy session.

Don't
bring your ex
along on your date.

Figuratively
or
literally.

Don't punish
your date
for what
your ex did.

Sharing too much about your ex
could just be pointing out
all the things that someone else
found wrong with you.

If you have to talk
about your ex,
give your date equal time
to talk about hers.

That way each of you
will be bored
only about half the time.

The height of the drama
is inversely proportional
to the depth
of your maturity.

Try not to
date the clone
of the woman
you just broke up with.

To build a
long-term relationship,
you two should have
slightly more in common
than the fact that you
(1) both like green houses;

(2) both had pets named "Fluffy" when you were kids;

(3) both learned to drive
on a stick shift;

(4) both fantasize about sending Rocco and Vinnie to blow up your ex's house, pet, car, or new girlfriend.

Don't hang around
with your ex-girlfriend's
girlfriends.

They *already* think you're crazy. And pretty soon, they'll convince you they're right.

No, you can't
date your therapist.

Therapy is one thing.
But your therapist *dating* you
is against the law.

You *can*,
on the other hand
(tee-hee),
date your ex's therapist
without having to report to
any licensing bureau.

What you report
to your ex
is up to you.

If you always bring a
friend with you to
singles events, you
won't ever be lonely.

But you'll probably
be single for
a very long time.

The best way to meet a
woman is to stop
looking for one.

Just as long as you don't stop going to places where a woman who also isn't looking can find you.

You will feel terrible
when you first hear that
your ex is dating again.

You will not believe the same is true for her.

A new date should not
be considered
"revenging" your ex.

Driving your new date
by your old ex's house
won't do anybody
any good.

If your ex got the couch
and chairs in the divorce,
go buy better looking
furniture.

She'll stop thinking she won,
and it will impress
your new dates.

Don't
keep
the bed.

DATING IS:

About the only
time your mother
was actually right
about the importance of
clean underwear.

Getting On With It

You can now sit up and take liquids.

It's time to get serious and get better at this lesbian dating thing. It's not like dating guys, only changing gender. You have years of conditioning to overcome.

You're looking for Ms. Right. Or even Ms. Right Away. So you have to face some realities. Here are some truths you'll need to know to get it right:

What To Bring:

- ✔ A Sense Of Humor
- ✔ Your Therapist's #
- ✔ Social Skills
- ✔ A Set Of Values
- ✔ Your Independence
- ✔ Your Own Money
- ✔ Your Own Car
- ✔ Marketable Skills

The first thing you have
to bring to the party
is yourself.

If you wouldn't want
to date you,
why should she?

Call
everyone.

Go
everywhere.

Dating services
are a wonderful way
to meet women
you wouldn't
want to date.

It's a numbers game.
Kiss a lot
of frogs.

If her personal ad says
she wants to take long walks on
romantic sunset beaches,
she's really looking
for hot sex.

If her personal ad says she's looking for hot sex, she's really after those sunset beach walks.

You will always seek in
someone else what you
wish for in yourself.

Be very careful
what you wish for.

You will say at least three
amazingly stupid things
in her presence the first
time you meet.

If the attraction is mutual,
she will not notice.
Until several years later.

If she's said "no" twice,
the answer really is "no."

Sometimes "no"
is just an answer,
not a personal rejection.

Your mother only
warned you about
calling *boys* first.

But she *was* right
about being
a good listener.

Lesbians are the
only ones who find
it necessary to
break up with a date.

There are no
anniversaries
in dating.

She will tell you in the first three weeks exactly what will go wrong.

Listen very carefully.

It is much easier to ask
the woman next to
the woman you want to
dance with, to dance.

Playing hard-to-get
could cost you ever
getting got.

If you believe
you'll never find anyone,
you and you alone will be
absolutely right.

Taking a lesbian date to a family reunion is tantamount to inviting psychotherapy.

You can't meet Ms. Right
by sitting at home
unless Ms. Right is
the FedEx driver.

If she says she
"isn't interested in dating,"
she means that she isn't
interested in dating
you.

Don't date
your employer
or your employee.

It never works out.

There is absolutely
nothing
casual
about sex.

Except the way that you have to talk about it with your new dates.

"I love you"
and
"The sex is great"
are NOT
the same thing.

DATING IS:

The only time you ever
feel an overwhelming
urge to shave
above the knee.

Just for the Fun of It

There have been several recently reported sightings of lesbians who dated other lesbians without moving in together. Though rare, these women appear to be dating just because they enjoy doing it.

They have short attention spans. And do not wish to make any changes in their living arrangements.

Many have never even been to a commitment ceremony. They merely see no reason to marry just to have occasional sex.

What To Bring:

- ✔ Your Own Vibrator
- ✔ Cab Fare
- ✔ A Big Black Book
- ✔ Dual-Control Electric Blanket
- ✔ Your Therapist's #
- ✔ Your Own Timetable
- ✔ Good Exit Lines

Many lesbians would date more than one available lesbian at a time.

If there were
that many available.

You *can* win 'em all.

Which is one of the problems.

Arousal, attraction,
complete panic, love,
and OD'ing on Hershey Bars
all feel pretty much
the same.

They do not, however,
call for exactly
the same response,
regardless of which one
you are enjoying.

Phone sex means never being off by even a millimeter.

Or missing a beat.

It is better to be
always charming
than it is to be
always right.

The longer the mystery,
the hotter the sex.

Date women who
are good at sex.
Marry women who are good
at being friends.

If you are really lucky,
these will be the same
woman.

A Women's Dance is no place to go to meet new women.

If you meet her in a bar, don't be surprised if she drinks.

If you are
dating more than one
woman at a time, remember:
this is what they invented
the word "darling" for.

If you date more than five women in one year, your reputation will exceed you.

Date the same woman more than three times, and all your friends will presume you are married.

So will the woman
you are dating.

It's a lot harder to turn a date
back into a friend.

Mercy dates
don't really
show any.

"Amusing" substitutes for
whole worlds of
"needs improvement."

Knowing the right people
can make almost anyone
look attractive.

Most women are
waiting for the
opportunity to say
"yes."

It's a good idea
to remember that
dating is supposed
to be fun.

If you didn't determine
beforehand
who is paying,
bring enough money.

If you don't have
enough money,
go someplace else.

If you're just dating for sex,
then you *both*
ought to be privy
to that information.

Dating is where most practicing skeptics get all their practice.

If it is not
–at some level–
about sex,
it is not
–at any level–
a date.

DATING IS:

That intensely
expensive time when
you have to decide
if *some*thing
is better than nothing.

Looking for Love

This is getting serious.

You want someone to feed the cats while you do the laundry. And you wouldn't mind testing your state's Defense of Marriage Act.

Now it's time to up the effort. And to learn from your previous mistakes.

Here are just a couple of things to keep in mind while you're letting your heart win:

What To Bring:

✔ Your Therapist's #

✔ A Fraction Of Yourself

✔ A Knot To Tie

✔ More Than Enough Rope

✔ A Melding Pot

✔ Shared Experience

✔ Merge Right Sign

✔ A Double Bed

145

A lesbian optimist is
someone who changes
the sheets and wears
colored underwear
on a first date.

You should try to come out
of the bedroom at least
with the changing
of the seasons.

All of your friends
will understand
why you are hibernating.

They will hold it against
you anyway.

Dating a woman who is
unhappier than you are
will not make either of
you happier.

Monogamists
and polygamists
will never convince
one another.

Children are best
served up to lovers
in small doses.

And vice versa.

You can't ever
take "I love you" back.

To win her,
woo the dog.

Date
in your
own mirror.

Eventually
opposites
repel.

While searching for Ms. Right,
you will also end up eating dinner
with Ms. Self-Righteous and
Ms. Always Right.

If it is really, really good, *none* of your friends will approve.

The pool of interesting
lesbians is always very
small and changes about
every eight and a half
minutes.

Some women are
worth waiting
nine minutes for.

Taking a lesbian date
to a family reunion
is tantamount to
admitting matrimony.

It cannot be true love
unless you, she,
and your beliefs about
the position of
the bathroom door,
all agree.

You will only fall in love
with someone on the Internet
who lives as far away
as possible.

One of you will move.

In a mere matter of years, those absolutely adorable idiosyncrasies you find so charming will drive you right up a wall.

Learn to take "yes"
for an answer.

The purpose of lesbian dating
is never to have to
do it again.

DATING IS:

What you schedule between burnout from activism, organizations, and long-term relationships.

Is There No End To This?

Okay, you dated. No fireworks. No U-Haul. No sunset to run off into.

Now what?

Do you really have to break up with someone you've just dated?

How?

What To Bring:

- ✔ A Firm Resolve
- ✔ A Conviction
- ✔ A Stiff Upper Lip
- ✔ Best Wishes
- ✔ A Rearview Mirror
- ✔ A Healthy Compassion
- ✔ Your Therapist's #
- ✔ A Crystal Ball

In a very small community,
it is necessary to be kind,
gentle, firm, and clear.
And with lesbians, the whole
world is a very small community.

The only dates you'll keep running into are the ones you leave rudely.

Saying "good-bye"
is an
either-or choice.

No matter how
loudly you say
"it isn't personal,"
it is.

Try to leave with grace.

Unless Grace is
your best friend's girlfriend.

Seeing each other every day,
sleeping together,
and not going out
with anyone else,
is
lesbian dating.

Name	Number	What I Liked Most

More Humor Books by Spinsters Ink

Ransacking the Closet, Yvonne Zipter $9.95
Roberts' Rules of Lesbian Break-Ups, Shelly Roberts $5.95
Roberts' Rules of Lesbian Dating, Shelly Roberts $5.95
Roberts' Rules of Lesbian Living, Shelly Roberts $5.95

Spinsters Ink titles are available at your local booksellers or by mail order through Spinsters Ink. A free catalog is available upon request. Please include $2.00 for the first title ordered and 50¢ for every title thereafter. Visa and Mastercard accepted. Please contact us for author appearances and signings.

Spinsters Ink
32 E. First St., #330
Duluth, MN 55802-2002
USA

218-727-3222 (Phone)   (Fax) 218-727-3119
(E-mail) spinster@spinsters-ink.com
(Website) http://www.spinsters-ink.com

Shelly was surprised to find herself doing research for her own benefit on the new rules of dating, so she decided to do it in a whole new world. Hotlanta.

The adventure continues as The Lesbian Philosopher General invades Atlanta for some lesbian 911.

Dating? She thought she was done with that forever. Hah!

Photo by Hazel Edlinger

Spinsters Ink was founded in 1978 to produce vital books for diverse women's communities. In 1986 we merged with Aunt Lute Books to become Spinsters/Aunt Lute. In 1990, the Aunt Lute Foundation became an independent, nonprofit publishing program. In 1992, Spinsters moved to Minnesota.

Spinsters Ink is committed to publishing novels and nonfiction works by women that deal with significant issues from a feminist perspective: books that not only name crucial issues in women's lives, but more importantly, encourage change and growth; books that help make the best in our lives more possible.